FIGHTER PILOTS
IN ACTION

BY TYLER OMOTH

The Child's World®
childsworld.com

Published by The Child's World®
1980 Lookout Drive • Mankato, MN 56003-1705
800-599-READ • www.childsworld.com

Photographs ©: Staff Sgt. Joe McFadden/U.S. Air Force, cover, 1; Stocktrek Images/Thinkstock, 5; Jeff Kraus/iStockphoto, 6; Fred Hayes/AP Images, 8; Sgt. Austin Long/U.S. Marine Corps, 9; Spc. Mitchell Murphy/U.S. Army, 10; Luca Bruno/AP Images, 13; 1st Lt. Alicia Lacy/U.S. Air National Guard, 14; Staff Sgt. Nathan G. Bevier/U.S. Air Force, 16; Shutterstock Images, 17; Staff Sgt. Benjamin Hughes/U.S. Air National Guard, 18; U.S. Air Force, 21; Master Sgt. Andy Dunaway/U.S. Air Force, 22; APTN/AP Images, 24; Airman 1st Class Mya M. Crosby/U.S. Air Force, 25; Staff Sgt. Aaron Allmon/U.S. Air Force, 26; David Guttenfelder/AP Images, 28

ISBN 9781503816299

LCCN 2016945641

Printed in the United States of America
PA02320

TABLE OF
CONTENTS

FAST FACTS

What's the Job?

- Fighter pilots fly military planes and helicopters in combat.

- They might have to engage the enemy in air-to-air combat or air-to-ground fights.

- Only the most elite pilots in the U.S. Air Force and U.S. Navy become fighter pilots.

- Fighter pilots must be in excellent physical shape and have very good eyesight.

The Dangers

- Fighter pilots fly extremely fast, putting great pressure on the pilot's body.

- Enemy planes try to shoot down fighter pilots.

- On the ground, missile launchers target fighter pilot planes and shoot surface-to-air missiles that can track their planes and kill them.

- If something goes wrong and the pilot needs to **eject** from the plane, the pilot can be hurt or killed by the ejection process. The pilot may also land in enemy territory.

Important Stats

- The U.S. Air Force has approximately 12,000 pilots and only 3,000 fighter pilots. However, the Air Force needs more fighter pilots. It offers more than $200,000 for qualified personnel to sign up for the job.

- In 2014, aircraft pilots and flight engineers ranked as the third-most-dangerous job in the United States. There were 63.2 deaths per 100,000 people employed in this job.

Chapter 1

SHOT DOWN

Scott O'Grady knew what he wanted to do after he finished college. He wanted to fly fighter jets. Scott attended a jet pilot training program at Sheppard Air Force Base in Texas. This training program prepares pilots to fly in combat missions. After completing his training there, Scott went on to train as a pilot in F-16 Fighting Falcon jets. These planes are fast and **maneuverable**. They are made for air-to-air combat. That is when two planes fight each other in the sky.

In the summer of 1995, Scott took to the skies. He was flying his F-16 in real combat action. It was during the Bosnian War (1992–1995). Scott was the **wingman** to Captain Bob Wright. Every morning, they met with commanding officers to go over all of the details of their mission. Then, the pilots had a few minutes to grab their survival equipment and get ready to go to their planes.

The pilots would be flying out to patrol a no-fly zone. These patrols make sure no unauthorized planes are flying in the area.

◀ **The F-16 Fighting Falcon was first developed in the 1970s.**

▲ Scott O'Grady stands in front of his F-16 Fighting Falcon.

This day, it was supposed to be a routine assignment. But for fighter pilots, every assignment is filled with danger.

Bosnian Serbs were on the opposite side of the conflict. The Serbs had moved their surface-to-air missile **batteries**. Scott and Captain Bob were flying above them. The pilots had no idea that the enemy weapons were there.

The Serbs fired two missiles at the planes. A high-pitched beep alerted the pilots to watch for the incoming missiles. But heavy cloud cover made it impossible to see the approaching missiles. With a flash and a bang, one missile exploded between the two planes. The pilots were unhurt. But not for long.

The second missile crashed into Scott's plane. The plane exploded into two pieces. As the plane started to fall from the sky, Scott did the only thing he could do in that situation. He hit the eject lever. Scott was launched away from the plane. He was now parachuting to the ground, deep into enemy territory.

▲ **Workers inspect an ejection seat to make sure it is in good condition.**

Scott was in the air for nearly 25 minutes as he slowly floated to the ground. His brightly colored parachute would make him an easy target if any enemy troops saw him. Luckily, he fell to the ground unseen. But he was not completely unharmed. His face and neck were burned from the explosion of his F-16.

As soon as Scott hit the ground, he tore free of his parachute. Then he grabbed some of his survival gear. He ran to some nearby woods to hide from view. Moments later, a man and a boy passed within 6 feet (1.8 m) of where Scott was hiding. He could hear their footsteps and see them moving. If Serbian troops saw him, they would probably kill him on the spot. When the people passed by Scott's hiding spot without noticing him, he breathed a sigh of relief.

For six days, Scott hid anywhere he could as he tried to make his way out of enemy territory. He tried to contact friendly troops with his radio at night. He knew that enemy troops would be less likely to detect him during those hours. Scott was in a wet, heavily wooded area. That environment made his boots heavy, and his footprints were obvious in the mud. Enemy helicopters flew by so close that Scott could see the pilots' faces. Remaining hidden was crucial to his survival.

◀ **Members of the U.S. Air Force practice survival techniques in case they are forced to eject from their aircraft.**

Scott didn't have any food. So he ate bugs and plants. He knew which ones were safe thanks to his survival training. Scott's emergency pack had water. But the emergency water ran out on the fourth day. Luckily, it started to rain. Scott was able collect more water in his survival **canteen**. But that same life-saving rain kept him soaked for days. He developed trench foot. That is a painful condition caused by constant wetness.

Scott continued moving toward friendly territory. He kept trying to call for help when he was able. He knew his team would be out on a search and rescue mission. Finally, on the sixth night, Scott's radio reached one of his squad members flying nearby.

Soon, four military helicopters were in the air. They headed to Scott's coordinates to pick him up. Fighter jets circled near the area in case the enemy noticed the rescue mission. At six o'clock in the morning, a helicopter touched down and found Scott waiting for rescue. He had a six-day beard and a pistol in his hand. He was ready to go home.

Scott O'Grady greets friends as he returns to his base. ▶

Chapter 2

COVER FLIGHT

In 1993, the U.S. military changed its rules. For the first time, women could fly planes in combat missions. For Kim Campbell, that decision meant her dream could come true. When she finished high school, Kim knew she wanted to be a pilot and serve her country.

In the U.S. Air Force, Kim spent years training to be a pilot. She flew an A-10 Thunderbolt II fighter plane. The A-10 was well equipped for night missions. Its **cockpit** had night-vision equipment. This equipment worked with the pilot's night-vision goggles to let her see in the dark. The A-10 could also fly and attack at slower speeds than most fighter jets. This slower speed made it easier to aim at targets on land. The plane could also provide cover for troops on the ground.

In April 2003, Kim was flying a mission over the skies of Baghdad, Iraq. Another fighter pilot flew an A-10 at Kim's side.

◀ **Many pilots refer to the A-10 by its nickname, the Warthog.**

▲ **A-10 planes often have shark mouths painted on their noses.**

The pilots were in Baghdad to attack an enemy command post. Kim's job was to take out the enemy's tanks and other vehicles with her A-10's heavy weaponry.

While they were on the way to their target, the pilots' plans changed. A nearby ground unit was taking heavy fire from enemy grenades. Kim and her wingman changed course immediately.

16

They hoped to aid the troops and take out the enemy threat. When they arrived, the pilots dipped below the cloud level. Now they could see who was friendly and who was the enemy.

▲ **Baghdad is a huge city with a population of more than seven million people.**

▲ The cockpit of an A-10 has a control stick and a large instrument panel.

From the skies, they let loose a blaze of heavy ammunition. The enemy troops kept firing. But they were no match for the A-10's high-powered guns and rockets. The pair of U.S. fighter planes made several passes over the enemy. Kim and her wingman tried to eliminate the threat to the friendly troops on the ground.

Suddenly, Kim heard a loud explosion. She felt her plane rock from the impact of a hit. Her plane started diving down and to the left. Kim knew that she was deep in enemy territory.

She didn't want to eject and parachute to the ground alone. So she tried to straighten out the jet. But the power that controlled her **wing flaps** had been damaged by the blast.

Kim switched her controls to manual. This switch allowed her to control her plane with a system of cables. The system was similar to a puppeteer making a puppet dance. Flying by hand control was a long shot, but it worked. The plane evened out. Kim climbed safely above the clouds.

Her wingman stayed close by her. He told Kim that her plane had one large hole the size of a football. The plane also had hundreds of small holes. The A-10 was designed to withstand damage and keep flying. But neither pilot was certain that Kim could make it nearly 300 miles (483 km) back to base.

Kim hoped her A-10 could hang on at least long enough to get back to friendly territory. Once there, she could safely eject. Kim flew toward the base. Her wingman kept watch for more damage or fire in Kim's plane. Despite the heavy damage, the plane handled well. After talking to her commanding officer, Kim decided to take it all the way back to the base.

Landing a fighter plane with all systems operating is a difficult task on its own. But Kim knew she could do it with only her manual controls.

As Kim got closer to the base, she could see emergency vehicles racing to the runway. They were prepared for a crash or an explosion.

Kim carefully approached the runway. She struggled to keep the plane level and to keep her speed on target. Her three wheels touched down, squealing on the paved runway. She applied the brake flaps and released an emergency parachute. The plane jerked violently as the parachute slowed it down. Finally, her heavily damaged fighter plane stopped. She had done it!

Kim breathed a sigh of relief. Men and women from the base ran towards her plane. They inspected the damage and made sure she was all right.

The next day, Kim's unit got a call. They were going on a search and rescue mission. A fellow A-10 pilot had been shot down by the enemy. Kim climbed into the cockpit of another plane and took off with the mission. She was a fighter pilot, and she had a job to do.

Kim Campbell looks at the damage on her plane. ▶

Chapter 3

DRAWING FIRE

After high school, Dan "Two Dogs" Hampton went into the U.S. Air Force for flight training. There he learned how to fly the F-16 Fighting Falcon jet. After his training, Dan flew on many missions and always came home safe. On March 19, 2003, he put on his suit and helmet and strapped in once again. The United States was at war with Iraq. The U.S. military wanted to start the conflict with an impressive attack. Dan and his team of "Wild Weasels" would be the first to fly into the combat zone.

His team had to fly into the outskirts of Baghdad, Iraq. There they would eliminate enemy missiles. This action would make it safe for U.S. bombers to come in and do major damage.

Dan took off at 5:30 a.m. with three other pilots. The sun was not up yet. Dan was happy to be attacking under the cover of darkness. He and his wingmen could use their night-vision technology to see fairly well. However, it would be hard for enemy troops on the ground to see them.

◀ **An F-16 Fighting Falcon flies over Iraq.**

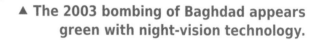

▲ **The 2003 bombing of Baghdad appears green with night-vision technology.**

The four pilots approached the target area in a rectangle formation. Then they split into two pairs of two jets. Each pair had a leader. The follower trailed 2 miles (3.2 km) behind. Dan was the leader of his pair. It didn't take long for their morning to become interesting.

Dan had nearly reached the combat zone. Suddenly, his plane's warning system started beeping. The enemy had fired a missile at him.

Four F-16 Fighting Falcons fly in formation. ▶

▲ A pilot releases countermeasures to confuse
enemy missiles.

Dan quickly located the building where the missile had come
from. Using his night-vision technology, he saw that the building
still glowed from the heat of the missile.

Dan fired his own missile at the building. Then he turned his
plane to avoid the missile that might be coming for him.

Within moments, he realized that the missile had not locked on to him. He was safe for now.

Dan's team continued to track down missile sites and take them out. His team was making the path safer for incoming bombers and troops. But it was not time to go back to their base yet. The Wild Weasels had a saying. They're the first in and last out. Dan and his squad would remain in the area to make sure everyone got out safely.

Then Dan's warning system started beeping again. Another missile was coming. This time it was right on his tail. Dan spun his F-16, diving away from the missile. With his left hand, he hit a button on his instrument panel. This button released **countermeasures** into the air behind him. With luck, they would draw the missile off target.

Dan pulled up on the throttle and leveled out the plane. His wingman yelled through the radio. The missile was still tracking him. Dan pointed the nose of his jet straight up at the stars. He continued to release more countermeasures.

By this point, Dan was flying blind. Neither he nor his wingman knew where the enemy missile was. Dan looked at his control panel. It showed a readout of everything in the sky, including jets, missiles, and countermeasures. Dan was relieved when saw that his last countermeasure had been destroyed.

The countermeasure had done its job perfectly, taking the missile that was meant for his plane.

Dan knew that he and his team were part of an important mission that morning. They had seen the explosions all throughout the city. Their attack had started the war with a decisive victory for the United States and its allies. The war had barely begun, but the United States and its allies were winning. And the Wild Weasels had cleared the way.

THINK ABOUT IT

- Fighter pilots face danger every time they take to the sky. They are also risking their lives to protect their country. What other ways can a person help his or her country?
- If a fighter pilot's plane is damaged, she might choose to eject and parachute to safety. Or she could try to fly the damaged plane back to base. How would you decide what to do?
- Teamwork is an important part of a fighter pilot's job. The leader flies in front, while the wingmen protect from behind. Would you rather lead or be a wingman? Why?

◀ **By mid-April 2003, ground troops had entered Baghdad.**

GLOSSARY

batteries (BAT-ur-eez): Batteries are groups of weapons or guns. The bombers aimed for the enemies' batteries.

canteen (kan-TEEN): A canteen is a container for water. The pilot filled his canteen with rainwater when he was behind enemy lines.

cockpit (KAHK-pit): A cockpit is the control area of a plane where the pilot sits. The cockpit has many controls that help the pilot fly the plane.

countermeasures (KOWN-tur-mezh-urz): Countermeasures are small objects that planes release to confuse the enemy's radar and missiles. The enemy's missile targeted the countermeasures and didn't hit the plane.

eject (i-JEKT): Eject means to be launched out of a plane's cockpit. When the jet was hit, the pilot had to eject.

maneuverable (muh-NOO-vur-uh-buhl): Maneuverable means able to be steered or directed easily. A maneuverable fighter jet can get out of the way of enemy missiles.

wing flaps (WING flaps): Wing flaps are movable parts on an airplane's wing that help to lift or slow the plane. The pilot adjusted the wing flaps to go higher.

wingman (WING-man): A wingman is a pilot who flies behind the leader to provide support and protection. The wingman saw enemy jets coming from the north.

TO LEARN MORE

Books

Corrigan, Jim. *Fighter Jets.* Greensboro, NC: Morgan Reynolds, 2014.

Lusted, Marcia Amidon. *Eyewitness to the Tuskegee Airmen.* Mankato, MN: Child's World, 2016.

Portman, Michael. *Fighter Jets.* New York: Gareth Stevens, 2013.

Web Sites

Visit our Web site for links about fighter pilots: childsworld.com/links

Note to Parents, Teachers, and Librarians: We routinely verify our Web links to make sure they are safe and active sites. So encourage your readers to check them out!

SELECTED BIBLIOGRAPHY

Almasy, Steve. "How Six Days Behind Enemy Lines Transformed Scott O'Grady." *CNN.* Turner Broadcasting System, 18 Dec. 2015. Web. 24 June 2016.

Haag, Jason. "Pilot Brings Battle-Damaged A-10 Home Safely." *Aircraft Resource Center.* Aircraft Resource Center, n.d. Web. 24 June 2016.

Hampton, Dan. *Viper Pilot: A Memoir of Air Combat.* New York: William Morrow, 2012. Print.

INDEX

ABOUT THE AUTHOR

Tyler Omoth has written more than 25 books for kids, covering a wide variety of topics. He has also published poetry and award-winning short stories. He loves sports and new adventures. Tyler currently lives in sunny Brandon, Florida, with his wife, Mary.